Let's Look at Sea Otters

Laura Hamilton Waxman

Lerner Publications Company

Minneapolis

Lerner Publications Company
A division of Lerner Publishing Group, Inc.
241 First Avenue North
Minneapolis, MN 55401 U.S.A.

Website address: www.lernerbooks.com

Library of Congress Cataloging-in-Publication Data

Waxman, Laura Hamilton.
    Let's look at sea otters / by Laura Hamilton Waxman.
        p.   cm. — (Lightning bolt books™ — Animal close-ups)
    Includes index.
    ISBN 978-0-8225-7896-3 (lib. bdg. : alk. paper)
    1. Sea otter—Juvenile literature. I. Title.
    QL737.C25W386 2011
    599.769'5—dc22   2007029225

Manufactured in the United States of America
1 — CG — 7/15/10

Contents

Sea otters

This furry animal is a sea otter. It lives in the sea.

Sea otters live near the coast.
They live in waters close
to land.

A sea otter floats
in the sea.

Some sea otters live off the coast of California. The days are often sunny. But the water is cold.

Sea otters play near the coast in California.

Many sea otters live near
Alaska. Alaska is much colder
than California. Alaska has
icy waters.

Staying Warm and Afloat

Sea otters are mammals. Mammals have fur or hair. Sea otters have the thickest fur of any mammal.

Thick fur keeps sea otters warm in the cold sea. Their fur grows in two layers. The outside layer has long hairs.

Can you see the long hairs on the sea otters' outside layer of fur?

The inside layer is soft and thick. It traps air around the sea otter's body. The air is like a warm blanket.

Dirty fur cannot trap air. A sea otter must groom its fur.

It must rub and scrub its fur clean.

Sea otters often groom and swim in rafts. A raft is a group of sea otters.

Sea otters mostly swim on their backs. They sleep on their backs too. Sleeping sea otters wrap themselves in kelp. This strong seaweed keeps them from floating away.

This sea otter is wrapped in kelp.

Hunting for Food

Splash! This sea otter is diving underwater. It is hunting for food.

A sea otter hunts a squid underwater.

A sea otter hunts for shellfish and other small animals. Hunted animals are called prey. Many of the prey live in underwater kelp forests.

A sea otter hunts prey at the bottom of the sea. It uses its strong back paws to swim to the bottom.

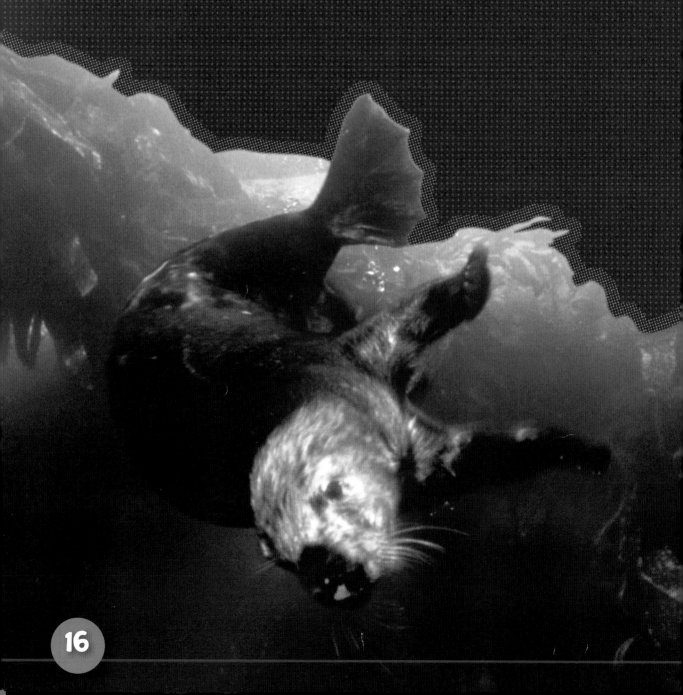

A sea otter can't always see in the dark water. It uses its whiskers and paws to feel for prey.

This sea otter uses its paws to feel for a sea urchin.

Mealtime

Yum! This sea otter is eating a tasty meal. Its tummy is its table.

Clams make a good meal for sea otters.

Its front paws hold the prey. Its sharp teeth tear out the meat. Some prey is too hard for teeth. What can a sea otter do?

This sea otter uses its teeth to eat crabmeat.

CRACK! A sea otter uses a
rock to break open hard shells.
It carries the rock on its chest.

A sea otter hits a
clam on a rock to
break it open.

Baby Sea Otters

Is this sea otter carrying a rock? No! It is carrying a baby sea otter. Baby sea otters are called pups.

Young pups cannot swim. They stay safe on top of their mothers.

A sea otter mother takes good care of her pup. She feeds it her milk. She grooms its fur. A pup's puffy fur helps it float.

A sea otter mother grooms her pup.

She also goes on short hunts to find prey for her pup. She eats some of the prey herself and shares the rest with her baby.

This sea otter is six weeks old.
It can swim and dive with its
mother.

She is teaching it how to hunt.

This older pup is growing up.
It can groom its own fur. It
can hunt its own prey.

An older pup hunts starfish in the sea.

A sea otter sets out on its own after six to eight months. It is ready for a life in the sea!

Sea Otter Range Map

RUSSIA

Bering Sea

Aleutian Islands

Prince William Sound

U.S.A.

AK

YT

NT

NU

BC

CANADA

AB

SK

MB

PACIFIC OCEAN

WA

MT

ND

MN

OR

ID

SD

WY

NV

UNITED STATES

IA

CA

UT

CO

NE

KS

MO

AZ

NM

OK

AR

TX

LA

MEXICO

■ Sea otter range

Sea Otter Diagram

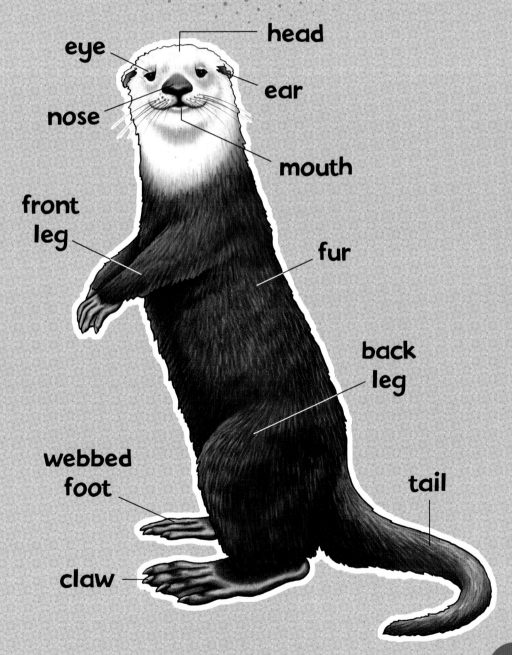

eye

head

nose

ear

mouth

front
leg

fur

back
leg

webbed
foot

tail

claw

Glossary

coast: land along the edge of the sea

groom: to keep fur clean

kelp: a tall seaweed that grows on the bottom of the ocean

mammal: an animal that has hair or fur and drinks its mother's milk when it is young

prey: hunted animals

pup: a baby sea otter

raft: a group of sea otters

Further Reading

Enchanted Learning: Sea Otter
http://www.enchantedlearning.com/subjects/
mammals/weasel/Seaotterprintout.shtml

Fleisher, Paul. *Ocean Food Webs.* Minneapolis:
Lerner Publication Company, 2008.

León, Vicki. *A Raft of Sea Otters.* Montrose, CA:
London Town Press, 2005.

Lockwood, Sophie. *Sea Otters.* Chanhassen, MN:
Child's World, 2006.

Meeker, Clare Hodgson. *Lootas, Little Wave Eater:
An Orphaned Sea Otter's Story.* Seattle: Sasquatch
Books, 2002.

Sea Otter Games and Interactives
http://www.montereybayaquarium.
org/efc/efc_otter/otter
_resources.aspx

Index

Photo Acknowledgments

The images in this book are used with the permission of: © Blaine Harrington III/ Alamy, p. 1; © Laura Romin & Larry Dalton/Alamy, p. 2; © Cusp/SuperStock, p. 4; © Nigel Hicks/Alamy, p. 5; © J. & C. Sohns/Animals Animals, p. 6; © Gerald & Buff Corsi/Visuals Unlimited, Inc., p. 7; © Richard R. Hansen/Photo Researchers, Inc., p. 8; © Michael Gore/FLPA/Minden Pictures, p. 9; © Thomas & Pat Leeson/Photo Researchers, Inc., pp. 10, 12, 20, 24, 30; © blickwinkel/Delpho/Alamy, p. 11; © Tom Mangelsen/naturepl.com, p. 13; © Norbert Wu/Minden Pictures, p. 14; © Doc White/ naturepl.com, p. 15; © OSF/Hall, H./Animals Animals, p. 16; © Jeff Foott/Discovery Channel Images/Getty Images, pp. 17, 19, 27; © Kirsten Wahlquist/Dreamstime.com, p. 18; © Bruce & Jan Lichtenberger/SuperStock, p. 21; © Steven J. Kazlowski/Alamy, p. 22; © Suzi Eszterhas/Minden Pictures, p. 23; © Hal Beral VWPics/SuperStock, p. 25; © Bates Littlehales/National Geographic/Getty Images, p. 26; © Laura Westlund/ Independent Picture Service, pp. 28, 29; © TUNS/Peter Arnold, Inc., p. 31.

Front cover: © Tier Und Naturfotografie J & C Sohns/Workbook Stock/Getty Images.